Socialism and man in Cuba

BY ERNESTO CHE GUEVARA

This article was written in the form of a letter to Carlos Quijano, editor of *Marcha*, a weekly published in Montevideo, Uruguay. It was first published in the March 12, 1965, issue of *Marcha*.

Dear compañero:

Though belatedly, I am completing these notes in the course of my trip through Africa, hoping in this way to keep my promise. I would like to do so by dealing with the theme set forth in the title above. I think it may be of interest to Uruguayan readers.

A common argument from the mouths of capitalist spokesmen, in the ideological struggle against socialism, is that socialism, or the period of building socialism into which we have entered, is characterized by the abolition of the individual for the sake of the state. I will not try to refute this argument solely on theoretical grounds, but rather to establish the facts as they exist in Cuba and then add comments of a general nature. Let me begin by broadly sketching the history of our revolutionary struggle before and after the taking of power.

As is well known, the exact date of the beginning of the revolutionary struggle—which would culminate in January 1959—was July 26, 1953. A group of men led by Fidel Castro attacked the Moncada garrison in Oriente Province on the morning of that day. The attack was a failure; the failure became a disaster; and the survivors ended up in prison, beginning the revolutionary struggle again after they were freed by an amnesty.

In this process, in which there was only the germ of socialism, man was a fundamental factor. We put our trust in him—individual, specific, with a first and last name—and the triumph or failure of the mission entrusted to him depended on his capacity for action.

Then came the stage of guerrilla struggle. It developed in two distinct environments: the people, the still sleeping mass that had to be mobilized; and its vanguard, the guerrillas, the motor force of the mobilization, the generator of revolutionary consciousness and militant enthusiasm. This vanguard was the catalyzing agent that created the subjective conditions necessary for victory.

Here again, in the framework of the proletarianization of our thinking, of this revolution that took place in our habits and our minds, the individual was the basic factor. Every one of the fighters of the Sierra Maestra who reached an upper rank in the revolutionary forces has a record of outstanding deeds to his credit. They attained their rank on this basis. It was the first heroic period, and in it they competed for the heaviest responsibilities, for the greatest dangers, with no other satisfaction than fulfilling a duty.

In our work of revolutionary education we frequently return to this instructive theme. In the attitude of our fighters could be glimpsed the man of the future.

On other occasions in our history the act of total dedication to the revolutionary cause was repeated. During the October [1962 missile] crisis and in the days of Hurricane Flora we saw exceptional deeds of valor and sacrifice performed by an entire people. Finding the method to perpetuate this heroic attitude in daily life is, from the ideological standpoint, one of our fundamental tasks.

In January 1959 the revolutionary government was established with the participation of various members of the treacherous bourgeoisie. The presence of the Rebel Army as the basic element of strength constituted the guarantee of power.

Serious contradictions developed right away. In the first instance, in February 1959, these were resolved when Fidel Castro assumed leadership of the government, taking the post of prime minister. This process culminated in July of the same year with the resignation under mass pressure of President Urrutia.

In the history of the Cuban revolution there now appeared a character, well defined in its features, who would systematically reappear: the mass.

This multifaceted being is not, as is claimed, the sum of elements of the same type (reduced, moreover, to that same type by the reigning system), which acts like a flock of sheep. It is true that it follows its leaders, basically Fidel Castro, without hesitation. But the degree to which he won this trust results precisely from having interpreted the people's desires and aspirations in their full meaning, and from the sincere struggle to fulfill the promises he made.

The mass participated in the agrarian reform and in the difficult task of the administration of state enterprises; it went through the heroic experience of Playa Girón [Bay of Pigs]; it was hardened in the battles against various bands of bandits armed by the CIA; it lived through one of the most important decisions of modern times during the October crisis; and today it continues to work for the building of socialism.

Viewed superficially, it might appear that those who speak of the subordination of the individual to the state are right. The mass carries out with matchless enthusiasm and discipline the tasks set by the government, whether in the field of the economy, culture, defense, sports, etc.

The initiative generally comes from Fidel or from the revolutionary high command and is explained to the people, who make it their own. In some cases the party and government take a local experience and generalize it, following the same procedure.

Nevertheless, the state sometimes makes mistakes. When one of these mistakes occurs, one notes a decline in collective enthusiasm due to the effect of a quantitative decrease in each of the elements that make up the mass. Work is paralyzed until it is reduced to insignificant amounts. It is time to make a correction. That is what happened in March 1962, as a result of the sectarian policy imposed on the party by Aníbal Escalante.

Clearly this mechanism is not enough to ensure a succession of sensible measures. A more structured connection with the mass is needed, and we must improve it in the course of the next years. But as far as initiatives originating in the upper strata of the government are concerned, we are currently utilizing the almost intuitive method of sounding out general reactions to the great problems we confront.

In this Fidel is a master. His own special way of fusing himself with the people can be appreciated only by seeing him in action. At the great public mass meetings one can observe something like the dialogue of two tuning forks whose vibrations interact, producing new sounds. Fidel and the mass begin to vibrate together in a dialogue of growing intensity until they reach the climax in an abrupt conclusion crowned by our cry of struggle and victory.

The difficult thing to understand for someone not living through the experience of the revolution is this close dialectical unity between the individual and the mass in which both are interrelated and, at the same time, in which the mass, as an aggregate of individuals, interacts with its leaders.

Some phenomena of this kind can be seen under capitalism, when politicians appear capable of mobilizing popular opinion. But when these are not genuine social movements—if they were, it would not be entirely correct to call them capitalist—they live only so long as the individual who inspires them, or until the harshness of capitalist society puts an end to the people's illusions.

In capitalist society man is controlled by a pitiless law usually beyond his comprehension. The alienated human specimen is tied to society as a whole by an invisible umbilical cord: the law of value. This law acts upon all aspects of his life, shaping his course and destiny.

The laws of capitalism, which are blind and are invisible to ordinary people, act upon the individual without his being aware of it. He sees only the vastness of a seemingly infinite horizon before him. That is how it is painted by capitalist propagandists who purport to draw a lesson from the example of Rockefeller—whether or not it is true—about the possibilities of success. The amount of poverty and suffering required for a Rockefeller to emerge, and the amount of depravity entailed in the accumulation of a fortune of such magnitude, are left out of the picture, and it is not always possible for the popular forces to make these concepts clear.

(A discussion of how the workers in the imperialist countries gradually lose the spirit of working-class internationalism due to a certain degree of complicity in the exploitation of the dependent countries, and how this at the same time weakens the combativity of the masses in the imperialist countries, would be appropriate here, but that is a theme which goes beyond the aim of these notes.)

In any case the road to success is pictured as beset with perils—perils that, it would seem, an individual with the proper qualities can overcome to attain the goal. The reward is seen in the distance; the way is lonely. Furthermore, it is a contest among wolves. One can win only at the cost of the failure of others.

I would now like to try to define the individual, the actor in this strange and moving drama of the building of socialism, in his dual existence as a unique being and as a member of society. I think the place to start is to recognize his quality of incompleteness, of being an unfinished product. The vestiges of the past are brought into the present in the individual consciousness, and a continual labor is necessary to eradicate them. The process is two-sided. On the one side, society acts through direct and indirect education; on the other, the individual submits himself to a conscious process of self-education.

The new society in formation has to compete fiercely with the past. This past makes itself felt not only in the individual consciousness—in which the residue of an education systematically oriented toward isolating the individual still weighs heavily—but also through the very character of this transition period in which commodity relations still persist. The commodity is the economic cell of capitalist society. So long as it exists its effects will make themselves felt in the organization of production and, consequently, in consciousness.

Marx outlined the transition period as resulting from the explosive transformation of the capitalist system destroyed by its own contradictions. In historical reality, however, we have seen that some countries that were weak limbs on the tree of imperialism were torn off first—a phenomenon foreseen by Lenin.

In these countries capitalism had developed sufficiently to make its effects felt by the people in one way or another. But it was not capitalism's internal contradictions that, having exhausted all possibilities, caused the system to explode. The struggle for liberation from a foreign oppressor; the misery caused by external events such as war, whose consequences privileged classes place on the backs of the exploited; liberation movements aimed at overthrowing neocolonial regimes—these are the usual factors in unleashing this kind of explosion. Conscious action does the rest.

A complete education for social labor has not yet taken place in these countries, and wealth is far from being within the reach of the masses through the simple process of appropriation. Underdevelopment, on the one hand, and the usual flight of capital, on the other, make a rapid transition without sacrifices impossible. There remains a long way to go in constructing the economic base, and the temptation is very great to follow the beaten track of material interest as the lever with which to accelerate development.

There is the danger that the forest will not be seen for the trees. The pipe dream that socialism can be achieved with the help of the dull instruments left to us by capitalism (the commodity as the economic cell, profitability, individual material interest as a lever, etc.) can lead into a blind alley. And you wind up there after having traveled a long distance with many crossroads, and it is hard to figure out just where you took the wrong turn. Meanwhile, the economic foundation that has been laid has done its work of undermining the development of conscious ness. To build communism it is necessary, simultaneous with the new material foundations, to build the new man.

That is why it is very important to choose the right instrument for mobilizing the masses. Basically, this instrument must be moral in character, without neglecting, however, a correct use of the material incentive—especially of a social character.

As I have already said, in moments of great peril it is easy to muster a powerful response to moral incentives. Retaining their effect, however, requires the development of a consciousness in which there is a new scale of values. Society as a whole must be converted into a gigantic school.

In rough outline this phenomenon is similar to the process by which capitalist consciousness was formed in its initial period. Capitalism uses force but it also educates people in the system. Direct propaganda is carried out by those entrusted with explaining the inevitability of class society, either through some theory of divine origin or a mechanical theory of natural law. This lulls the masses, since they see themselves as being oppressed by an evil against which it is impossible to struggle.

Next comes hope of improvement—and in this, capitalism differed from the earlier caste systems, which offered no way out. For some people, the principle of the caste system will remain in effect: The reward for the obedient is to be transported after death to some fabulous other world where, according to the old beliefs, good people are rewarded. For other people there is this innovation: Class divisions are determined by fate, but individuals can rise out of their class through work, initiative, etc. This process, and the myth of the self-made man, are profoundly hypocritical: it is the self-serving effort to turn a lie into the truth.

In our case direct education acquires a much greater importance. The explanation is convincing because it is true; no subterfuge is needed. It is carried on by the state's educational apparatus as a function of general, technical, and ideological education through such agencies as the Ministry of Education and the party's informational apparatus. Education takes hold among the masses and the foreseen new attitude tends to become a habit. The masses continue to make it their own and to influence those who have not yet educated themselves. This is the indirect form of educating the masses, as powerful as the other.

But the process is a conscious one. The individual continually feels the impact of the new social power and perceives that he does not entirely measure up to its standards. Under the pressure of indirect education, he tries to adjust himself to a situation that he feels is right and that his own lack of development had prevented him from reaching previously. He educates himself.

In this period of the building of socialism we can see the new man being born. His image is not yet completely finished—it never will be, since the process goes forward hand in hand with the development of new economic forms.

Aside from those whose lack of education makes them take the solitary road toward satisfying their own personal ambitions, there are those—even within this new panorama of a unified march forward—who have a tendency to walk separate from the masses accompanying them. What is important, however, is that each day men are acquiring ever more consciousness of the need for their incorporation into society and, at the same time, of their importance as the motor of that society.

They no longer travel completely alone over lost roads toward distant aspirations. They follow their vanguard, consisting of the party, the advanced workers, the advanced men who walk in unity with the masses and in close communion with them. The vanguards have their eyes fixed on the future and its reward, but it is not a vision of something for the individual. The prize is the new society in which men will have different characteristics: the society of communist man.

The road is long and full of difficulties. At times we lose our way and must turn back. At other times we go too fast and separate ourselves from the masses. Sometimes we go too slow and feel the hot breath of those treading at our heels. In our zeal as revolutionists we try to move ahead as fast as possible, clearing the way. But we know we must draw our nourishment from the mass and that it can advance more rapidly only if we inspire it by our example.

Despite the importance given to moral incentives, the fact that there remains a division into two main groups (excluding, of course, the minority that for one reason or another does not participate in the building of socialism) indicates the relative lack of development of social consciousness. The vanguard group is ideologically more advanced than the mass; the latter understands the new values, but not sufficiently. While among the former there has been a qualitative change that enables them to make sacrifices in their capacity as an advance guard, the latter see only part of the picture and must be subject to incentives and pressures of a certain intensity. This is the dictatorship of the proletariat operating not only on the defeated class but also on individuals of the victorious class.

All of this means that for total success a series of mechanisms, of revolutionary institutions, is needed. Along with the image of the multitudes marching toward the future comes the concept of institutionalization as a harmonious set of channels, steps, restraints, and well-oiled mechanisms that facilitate the advance, that facilitate the natural selection of those destined to march in the vanguard, and that bestow rewards on those who fulfill their duties and punishments on those who commit a crime against the society that is being built.

This institutionalization of the revolution has not yet been achieved. We are looking for something new that will permit a complete identification between the government and the community in its entirety, something appropriate to the special conditions of the building of socialism, while avoiding to the utmost a transplanting of the commonplaces of bourgeois democracy— such as legislative chambers, for example—into the society in formation.

Some experiments aimed at the gradual institutionalization of the revolution have been made, but without undue haste. The greatest brake has been our fear lest any appearance of formality might separate us from the masses and from the individual, might make us lose sight of the ultimate and most important revolutionary aspiration: to see man liberated from his alienation.

Despite the lack of institutions, which must be overcome gradually, the masses are now making history as a conscious collection of individuals fighting for the same cause. Man under socialism, despite his apparent standardization, is more complete. Despite the lack of a perfect mechanism for it, his opportunities for expressing himself and making himself felt in the social organism are infinitely greater.

It is still necessary to deepen his conscious participation, individual and collective, in all the mechanisms of management and production, and to link this to the idea of the need for technical and ideological education, so that he sees how closely interdependent these processes are and how their advancement is parallel. In this way he will reach total consciousness of his social being, which is equivalent to his full realization as a human creature, once the chains of alienation are broken.

This will be translated concretely into the reconquering of his true nature through liberated labor, and the expression of his own human condition through culture and art.

In order for him to develop in the first way, work must acquire a new status. Man-as-a-commodity ceases to exist, and a system is installed that establishes a quota for the fulfillment of his social duty. The means of production belong to society, and the machine is merely the trench where duty is fulfilled.

Man begins to free his thinking of the annoying fact that he needs to work to satisfy his animal needs. He starts to see himself reflected in his work and to understand his full stature as a human being through the object created, through the work accomplished. Work no longer entails surrendering a part of his being in the form of labor power sold, which no longer belongs to him, but represents an emanation of himself, a contribution to the common life in which he is reflected, the fulfillment of his social duty.

We are doing everything possible to give work this new status of social duty and to link it on the one side with the development of technology, which will create the conditions for greater freedom, and on the other side with voluntary work based on the Marxist appreciation that man truly reaches his full human condition when he produces without being compelled by physical necessity to sell himself as a commodity.

Of course, there are still coercive aspects to work, even when it is voluntary. Man has not transformed all the coercion that surrounds him into conditioned reflexes of a social character, and in many cases he still produces under the pressures of his environment. (Fidel calls this moral compulsion.) He still needs to undergo a complete spiritual rebirth in his attitude toward his own work, freed from the direct pressure of his social environment, though linked to it by his new habits. That will be communism.

The change in consciousness does not take place automatically, just as change in the economy does not take place automatically. The alterations are slow and are not rhythmic; there are periods of acceleration, ones that are slower, and even retrogressions.

Furthermore we must take into account, as I pointed out before, that we are not dealing with a period of pure transition, as Marx envisaged it in his *Critique of the Gotha Programme*, but rather with a new phase unforeseen by him: an initial period of the transition to communism, or of the construction of socialism. It is taking place in the midst of violent class struggles, and with elements of capitalism within it that obscure a complete understanding of its essence.

If we add to this the scholasticism that has held back the development of Marxist philosophy and impeded a systematic treatment of the transition period, whose political economy has not been developed, we must agree that we are still in diapers and that it is necessary to devote ourselves to investigating all the principal characteristics of this period before elaborating an economic and political theory of greater scope.

The resulting theory will, no doubt, put great stress on the two pillars of the construction of socialism: the education of the new man and the development of technology. Much remains to be done in regard to both, but delay is least excusable in regard to the concept of technology as a basic foundation since this is not a question of going forward blindly but of following a long stretch of road already opened up by the world's more advanced countries. This is why Fidel pounds away with such insistence on the need for the technological and scientific training of our people and especially of its vanguard.

In the field of ideas that do not lead to activities involving production, it is easier to see the division between material and spiritual necessity. For a long time man has been trying to free himself from alienation through culture and art. While he dies every day during the eight or more hours in which he functions as a commodity, he comes to life afterward in his spiritual creations. But this remedy bears the germs of the same sickness: it is a solitary individual seeking harmony with the world. He defends his individuality, which is oppressed by the environment, and reacts to aesthetic ideas as a unique being whose aspiration is to remain immaculate.

It is nothing more than an attempt to escape. The law of value is no longer simply a reflection of the relations of production; the monopoly capitalists—even while employing purely empirical methods—surround it with a complicated scaffolding that turns it into a docile servant. The superstructure demands a kind of art that the artist has to be educated in. Rebels are subdued by the machine, and only exceptional talents may create their own work. The rest become shamefaced hirelings or are crushed.

A school of artistic inquiry is invented, which is said to be the definition of freedom, but this "inquiry" has its limits, imperceptible until we clash with them, that is, until the real problems of man and his alienation arise. Meaningless anguish or vulgar amusement thus become convenient safety valves for human anxiety. The idea of using art as a weapon of protest is combated.

Those who play by the rules of the game are showered with honors—such honors as a monkey might get for performing pirouettes. The condition is that you not try to escape from the invisible cage.

When the revolution took power there was an exodus of those who had been completely housebroken. The rest—whether they were revolutionaries or not—saw a new road. Artistic inquiry experienced a new impulse. The paths, however, had already been more or less laid out, and the escapist concept hid itself behind the word "freedom." This attitude was often found even among the revolutionaries themselves, a reflection in their consciousness of bourgeois idealism.

In countries that have gone through a similar process, attempts have been made to combat such tendencies by an exaggerated dogmatism. General culture was virtually a taboo, and the acme of cultural aspiration was declared to be the formally exact representation of nature. This was later transformed into a mechanical representation of the social reality they wanted to show: the ideal society, almost without conflicts or contradictions, that they sought to create.

Socialism is young and has its mistakes. We revolutionaries often lack the knowledge and intellectual daring needed to meet the task of developing the new man with methods different from the conventional ones—and the conventional methods suffer from the influences of the society that created them. (Again the theme of the relationship between form and content is posed.) Disorientation is widespread, and we are absorbed by the problems of material construction. There are no artists of great authority who at the same time have great revolutionary authority. The men of the party must take this task in hand and seek attainment of the main goal: to educate the people.

What is sought then is simplification, something everyone can understand, something functionaries understand. True artistic inquiry ends, and the problem of general culture is reduced to taking some things from the socialist present and some from the dead (therefore, not dangerous) past. Thus socialist realism arises upon the foundations of the art of the last century.

But the realistic art of the nineteenth century also has a class character, more purely capitalist perhaps than this decadent art of the twentieth century that reveals the anguish of alienated man. In the field of culture capitalism has given all that it had to give, and nothing remains but the stench of a corpse, today's decadence in art.

But why try to find the only valid prescription in the frozen forms of socialist realism? We cannot counterpose "freedom" to socialist realism, because the former does not yet exist and will not exist until the complete development of the new society. But we must not, from the pontifical throne of realism-at-all-costs, condemn all art forms since the first half of the nineteenth century, for we would then fall into the Proudhonian mistake of going back to the past, of putting a straitjacket on the artistic expression of the man who is being born and is in the process of making himself.

What is needed is the development of an ideological-cultural mechanism that permits both free inquiry and the uprooting of the weeds that multiply so easily in the fertilized soil of state subsidies.

In our country the error of mechanical realism has not appeared, but rather its opposite. And that is so because the need for the creation of a new man has not been understood, a new man who would represent neither the ideas of the nineteenth century nor those of our own decadent and morbid century.

What we must create is the man of the twenty-first century, although this is still a subjective aspiration, not yet systematized. This is precisely one of the fundamental objectives of our study and our work. To the extent that we achieve concrete successes on a theoretical plane—or, vice versa, to the extent that we draw theoretical conclusions of a broad character on the basis of our concrete research—we will have made a valuable contribution to Marxism-Leninism, to the cause of humanity.

By reacting against the man of the nineteenth century we have relapsed into the decadence of the twentieth century. It is not a very grave error, but we must overcome it lest we open a wide breach for revisionism.

The great multitudes continue to develop. The new ideas are gaining a good momentum within society. The material possibilities for the integrated development of absolutely all members of society make the task much more fruitful. The present is a time of struggle; the future is ours.

To sum up, the fault of many of our artists and intellectuals lies in their original sin: they are not truly revolutionaries. We can try to graft the elm tree so that it will bear pears, but at the same time we must plant pear trees. New generations will come that will be free of original sin. The probabilities that great artists will appear will be greater to the degree that the field of culture and the possibilities for expression are broadened.

Our task is to prevent the current generation, torn asunder by its conflicts, from becoming perverted and from perverting new generations. We must not create either docile servants of official thought, or "scholarship students" who live at the expense of the state—practicing freedom in quotation marks. Revolutionaries will come who will sing the song of the new man in the true voice of the people. That is a process that takes time.

In our society the youth and the party play a big part.

The former is especially important because it is the malleable clay from which the new man can be built without any of the old vestiges. The youth are treated in accordance with our aspirations. Their education is every day more complete, and we are not forgetting about their integration into work from the outset. Our scholarship students do physical work during their vacations or along with their studying. Work is a reward in some cases, a means of education in others, but it is never a punishment. A new generation is being born.

The party is a vanguard organization. It is made up of the best workers, who are proposed for membership by their fellow workers. It is a minority, but it has great authority because of the quality of its cadres. Our aspiration is for the party to become a mass party, but only when the masses have reached the level of the vanguard, that is, when they are educated for communism.

Our work constantly aims at this education. The party is the living example. Its cadres must teach hard work and sacrifice. By their action, they must lead the masses to the completion of the revolutionary task, and this involves years of hard struggle against the difficulties of construction, class enemies, the maladies of the past, imperialism.

I would now like to explain the role played by the individual, by man as an individual within the masses who make history. This is our experience; it is not a prescription.

Fidel gave the revolution its impulse in the first years, and also its leadership. He always set its tone. But there is a good group of revolutionaries who are developing along the same road as the central leader. And there is a great mass that follows its leaders because it has faith in them. It has faith in them because they have known how to interpret its aspirations.

It is not a matter of how many kilograms of meat one has to eat, nor of how many times a year someone can go to the beach, nor how many pretty things from abroad you might be able to buy with present-day wages. It is a matter of making the individual feel more complete, with much more internal richness and much more responsibility.

The individual in our country knows that the glorious period in which he happens to live is one of sacrifice; he is familiar with sacrifice. The first ones came to know it in the Sierra Maestra and wherever they fought; afterward all of Cuba came to know it. Cuba is the vanguard of Latin America and must make sacrifices because it occupies the post of advance guard, because it shows the masses of Latin America the road to full freedom.

Within the country the leadership has to carry out its vanguard role. And it must be said with all sincerity that in a real revolution, to which one gives his all and from which one expects no material reward, the task of the vanguard revolutionary is at one and the same time magnificent and agonizing.

At the risk of seeming ridiculous, let me say that the true revolutionary is guided by great feelings of love. It is impossible to think of a genuine revolutionary lacking this quality. Perhaps it is one of the great dramas of the leader that he must combine a passionate spirit with a cold intelligence and make painful decisions without flinching. Our vanguard revolutionaries must make an ideal of this love of the people, of the most sacred causes, and make it one and indivisible. They cannot descend, with small doses of daily affection, to the level where ordinary men put their love into practice.

The leaders of the revolution have children just beginning to talk, who are not learning to say "daddy." They have wives who must be part of the general sacrifice of their lives in order to take the revolution to its destiny. The circle of their friends is limited strictly to the circle of comrades in the revolution. There is no life outside of it.

In these circumstances one must have a big dose of humanity, a big dose of a sense of justice and truth in order not to fall into dogmatic extremes, into cold scholasticism, into an isolation from the masses. We must strive every day so that this love of living humanity is transformed into actual deeds, into acts that serve as examples, as a moving force.

The revolutionary, the ideological motor force of the revolution within his party, is consumed by this uninterrupted activity that comes to an end only with death, unless the construction of socialism is accomplished on a world scale. If his revolutionary zeal is blunted when the most urgent tasks have been accomplished on a local scale and he forgets about proletarian internationalism, the revolution he leads will cease to be a driving force and sink into a comfortable drowsiness that imperialism, our irreconcilable enemy, will utilize to gain ground. Proletarian internationalism is a duty, but it is also a revolutionary necessity. This is the way we educate our people.

Of course there are dangers in the present situation, and not only that of dogmatism, not only that of freezing the ties with the masses midway in the great task. There is also the danger of the weaknesses we can fall into. If a man thinks that dedicating his entire life to the revolution means that in return he should not be distracted by such worries as that his child lacks certain things, that his children's shoes are worn out, that his family lacks some necessity, then with this reasoning he opens his mind to infection by the germs of future corruption.

In our case we have maintained that our children should have or should go without those things that the children of the common man have or go without, and that our families should understand this and struggle for it to be that way. The revolution is made through man, but man must forge his revolutionary spirit day by day.

Thus we march on. At the head of the immense column—we

are neither ashamed nor afraid to say it—is Fidel. After him come the best cadres of the party, and immediately behind them, so close that we feel its tremendous force, comes the people in its entirety, a solid structure of individualities moving toward a common goal, individuals who have attained consciousness of what must be done, men who fight to escape from the realm of necessity and to enter that of freedom.

This great throng organizes itself; its organization is a result of its consciousness of the necessity of this organization. It is no longer a dispersed force, divisible into thousands of fragments thrown into the air like splinters from a hand grenade, trying by any means to achieve some protection from an uncertain future, in desperate struggle with their fellows.

We know that sacrifices lie ahead and that we must pay a price for the heroic fact that we are, as a nation, a vanguard. We, as leaders, know that we must pay a price for the right to say that we are at the head of a people that is at the head of Latin America. Each and every one of us punctually pays his quota of sacrifice, conscious of being rewarded with the satisfaction of fulfilling a duty, conscious of advancing with everyone toward the new man visible on the horizon.

Allow me to draw some conclusions:

We socialists are freer because we are more complete; we are more complete because we are freer.

The skeleton of our complete freedom is already formed. The flesh and the clothing are lacking; we will create them.

Our freedom and its daily sustenance are paid for in blood and sacrifice.

Our sacrifice is conscious: an installment payment on the freedom that we are building.

The road is long and in part unknown. We know our limitations. We will create the man of the twenty-first century—we, ourselves.

We will forge ourselves in daily action, creating a new man with a new technology.

The individual plays a role in mobilizing and leading the masses insofar as he embodies the highest virtues and aspirations of the people and does not wander from the path.

Clearing the way is the vanguard group, the best among the good, the party.

The basic clay of our work is the youth. We place our hope in them and prepare them to take the banner from our hands.

If this inarticulate letter clarifies anything, it has accomplished the objective that motivated it. Receive our ritual greeting—which is like a handshake or an "Ave María Purísima":

Patria o muerte! [Homeland or death]

Che's ideas are absolutely relevant today

BY FIDEL CASTRO

This speech was given on October 8, 1987, at the main ceremony marking the twentieth anniversary of Guevara's death. It was held at a newly completed electronic components factory in the city of Pinar del Río.

Nearly twenty years ago, on October 18, 1967, we met in the Plaza of the Revolution with a huge crowd to honor Compañero Ernesto Che Guevara. Those were very bitter, very difficult days when we received news of the developments in Vado del Yeso, in the Yuro Ravine, when news agencies reported Che had fallen in battle.

It didn't take long to realize that those reports were absolutely correct, for they consisted of news items and photos that proved it beyond doubt. For several days the news was coming in, until with all that information in hand—although many of the details we know today were not known at the time—we held the large mass rally, the solemn ceremony in which we paid our last respects to the fallen compañero.

Nearly twenty years have passed since then, and now, on October 8, we are marking the date he fell in battle. According to reliable reports we have now, he was actually murdered the following day, after having been captured unarmed and wounded; his weapon had been rendered useless in battle. That's why it has become a tradition to commemorate that dramatic event on October 8.

The first year passed and then five, ten, fifteen, and now twenty years, and it was necessary to recall the historic dimensions of that development, and particularly the man. Thus in a natural way, rather than a very deliberate or pondered way, the entire people have been recalling the date in recent months. It was possible to commemorate the twentieth anniversary on a solemn note as we have seen here today: the playing of taps, the anthem, the magnificent poem by Nicolás Guillén, which rang out with the same voice we heard twenty years ago.

I could try to give a very solemn, grandiloquent speech, perhaps a written speech, but in these times the pressure of work barely leaves a minute free for thinking more carefully about all those events and the things I could say here, let alone for writing a speech.

That's why I'd prefer to recall Che, share my thoughts with you, because I've thought a lot about Che.

I did an interview, part of which was made public yesterday in our country, in answer to the questions of an Italian journalist who had me in front of the television cameras nearly sixteen hours straight—actually, they were movie, not TV cameras, because in order to get a better image in everything he did, he didn't use videocassettes, some of which last two hours, but rather movie cameras. He'd change reels every twenty or twenty-five minutes, and so it was quite an exhausting interview. We should have taken three days to do it, but we had to do it in one because there was no more time. We started before noon on a Sunday and finished at 5:00 a.m. the following day. There were more than 100 questions. Among the variety of subjects and themes, the journalist was very interested in talking about Che, and between 3:00 and 4:00 a.m. we got to the subject. I made an effort to answer each of his questions, and I made a special effort to summarize my memories of Che.

I told him how I felt, and I think many compañeros feel the same way, regarding Che's permanent presence. We must keep in mind the special relationship with Che, the affection, the fraternal bonds of comradeship, the united struggle over nearly twelve years, from the moment we met in Mexico until the end, a period rich in historic events, some of which have been made public only in the last couple of days.

It was a period filled with heroic and glorious deeds, from the time Che joined us to go on the *Granma* expedition, the landing, the setbacks, the most difficult days, the resumption of the struggle in the mountains, rebuilding an army virtually from scratch, the first clashes, and the last battles.

Then the intense period that followed the victory of the revolution: the first revolutionary laws, in which we were absolutely loyal to the commitments we'd made to the people, carrying out a really radical transformation in the life of the country. There were the things that followed, one after another, such as the start of imperialist hostility; the blockade; the slander campaigns against the revolution as soon as we started to do justice to the criminals and thugs who had murdered thousands of our fellow citizens; the economic blockade; the Girón invasion; the proclamation of the socialist nature of the revolution; the struggle against the mercenaries; the October crisis; the first steps in the construction of socialism when there was nothing—neither experience nor cadres nor engineers nor economists and hardly any technicians, when we were left almost without doctors because 3,000 of the 6,000 doctors in the country left.

Then came the First and Second Declarations of Havana, the start of the isolation imposed on our country, the collective rupture of diplomatic relations by all Latin American governments except Mexico. It was a period in which, along with all these developments, we had to organize the economy of the country. It was a relatively brief but fruitful period replete with unforgettable events.

It must be kept in mind that Che persisted in an old desire, an old idea: to return to South America, to his country, to make the revolution based on the experience he'd gained in our country. We should recall the clandestine way in which his departure had to be organized, the barrage of slanders against the revolution, when there was talk of conflicts, of differences with Che, that Che had disappeared. It was even said that he had been murdered because of splits in the ranks of the revolution.

Meanwhile, the revolution calmly and firmly endured the ferocious attack, because over and above the irritation and bitterness caused by those campaigns, the important thing was for Che to be able to fulfill his goals; the important thing was to ensure his safety and that of the compatriots with him on his historic missions.

In the interview I explained the origin of that idea, how when he joined us he had set only one condition: that once the revolution was made, when he wanted to return to South America he would not be prevented from doing so for reasons of state or for the state's convenience, that he would not be held back. We told him he could go ahead and that we would support him. He would remind us of this pledge every so often until the time came when he decided it was time to leave.

Not only did we keep the promise of agreeing to his departure, but we gave him all the help we could. We tried to delay the departure a little. We gave him other tasks to enrich his guerrilla experience, and we tried to create a minimum of conditions so that he would not have to go through the most difficult stage of the first days of organizing a guerrilla force, something we knew full well from our own experience.

We were well aware of Che's talent, his experience, and his role. He was a cadre suited to major strategic tasks and we felt it might be better if other compañeros undertook the initial organizational work and that he join at a more advanced stage in the process. This also fit in with our policy during the war of saving cadres, as they distinguished themselves, for increasingly important and strategic assignments. We did not have many experienced cadres, and as they distinguished themselves we would not send them out every day with a squad to ambush; rather, we gave them more important tasks in keeping with their ability and experience.

Thus, I remember that during the days of Batista's final offensive in the Sierra Maestra mountains against our militant but small forces, the most experienced cadres were not in the front lines; they were assigned strategic leadership assignments and saved for our devastating counterattack. It would have been pointless to put Che, Camilo [Cienfuegos], and other compañeros who had participated in many battles at the head of a squad. We held them back so that they could subsequently lead columns that would undertake risky missions of great importance, and it was then that we did send them into enemy territory with full responsibility and awareness of the risks, as in the case of the invasion of Las Villas led by Camilo and Che, an extraordinarily difficult assignment that required men of great experience and authority as column commanders, men capable of reaching the goal.

In line with this reasoning, and considering the objectives, perhaps it would have been better if this principle had been observed and Che had joined at a later stage. It really was not so critical for him to handle everything right from the start. But he was impatient, very impatient really. Some Argentine comrades had been killed in the initial efforts he had made years before, including Ricardo Massetti, the founder of Prensa Latina. He remembered that often and was really impatient to start to participate personally in the work.

As always, we respected our commitments and his views, for our relationship was always based on absolute trust, absolute brotherhood, regardless of our ideas about what would be the right time for him to join in. And so we gave him all the help and all the facilities possible to start the struggle.

Then news came of the first clashes and contact was completely lost. The enemy detected the initial stage of organization of the guerrilla movement, and this marked the start of a period lasting many months in which almost the only news we received was what came via international news dispatches, and we had to know how to interpret them. But that's something our revolution has become very experienced at: determining when a report is reliable or when it is made up, false.

I remember, for example, when a dispatch came with the news of the death of Joaquín's group (his real name was Vilo Acuña).[*] When we analyzed it, I immediately concluded that it was true; this was because of the way they described how the group had been eliminated while crossing a river. Because of our own guerrilla experience, because of what we had lived through, we knew how a small guerrilla group can be done away with. We knew the few, exceptional ways such a group can be destroyed.

When it was reported that a peasant had made contact with the army and provided detailed information on the location and plans of the group, which was looking for a way to cross the river; how the army set up an ambush on the other bank at a spot on the route the same peasant had told the guerrilla fighters to use; the way the army opened fire in midstream, there was no doubt as to the truth of the explanation. If the writers of false reports, which came in often, tried to do it again, it was impossible to admit that they, who were always so clumsy in their lies, would have had enough intelligence and experience to make up the exact and only circumstances in which the group could be eliminated. That's why we concluded the report was true.

Long years of revolutionary experience had taught us to decipher dispatches and tell the difference between the truth and

[*] On April 17, 1967, the guerrilla unit in Bolivia was divided in two, with the main group led by Guevara and the rear guard of seventeen fighters under the command of Joaquín (Juan Vitalio Acuña). Although the separation was supposed to last for only a few days, the two groups lost contact with each other permanently. On August 31, the remnant of Joaquín's group fell into an ambush and was annihilated.

falsehood of each development, although, of course, there are other things to keep in mind when making a judgment. But that was the type of information we had about the situation until the news of Che's death arrived.

As we have explained, we had hopes that even with only twenty men left, even in a very difficult situation, the guerrillas still had a chance. They were headed toward an area where sectors of the peasants were organized, where some good Bolivian cadres had influence, and until that moment, until almost the very end, there was a chance that the movement could be consolidated and could develop.

But the circumstances in which my relationship with Che developed were so unique—the almost unreal history of the brief but intense saga of the first years of the revolution when we were used to making the impossible possible—that, as I explained to that journalist, one had the permanent impression that Che had not died, that he was still alive. Since his was such an exemplary personality, so unforgettable, so familiar, it was difficult to resign oneself to the idea of his death.

Sometimes I would dream—all of us dream of things related to our lives and struggles—that I saw Che, that he returned, that he was alive. How often this happened! I told the journalist that these are feelings you seldom talk about, but they give an idea of the impact of Che's personality and also of the extraordinary degree to which he really lives on, almost as if his was a physical presence, with his ideas and deeds, with his example and all the things he created, with his continued relevance and the respect for him not only in Latin America but in Europe and all over the world.

As we predicted on October 18, twenty years ago, he became a symbol for all the oppressed, for all the exploited, for all patriotic and democratic forces, for all revolutionaries. He became a permanent and invincible symbol.

We feel Che's presence for all these reasons, because of this real force that he still has today which, even though twenty years have gone by, exists in the spirit of all of us, when we hear the poem, when we hear the anthem, or the bugle is sounded before a moment's silence, when we open our newspapers and see photographs of Che during different stages of his life, his image, so well known throughout the world—because it has to be said that Che not only had all the virtues and all the human and moral qualities to be a symbol, he also had the appearance of a symbol, the image of a symbol: his look, the frankness and strength of his look; his face, which reflects character, irrepressibly determined for action, at the same time showing great intelligence and great purity—when we look at the poems that have been written, the episodes that are recounted, and the stories that are repeated, we feel the reality of Che's relevance, of his presence.

It's not strange if one feels Che's presence not only in everyday life, but even in dreams if one imagines that he is alive, that Che is in action and that he never died. In the end we must reach the conclusion that to all intents and purposes in the life of our revolution Che never died, and in the light of what has been done, he is more alive than ever, has more influence than ever, and is a more powerful opponent of imperialism than ever.

Those who disposed of his body so that he would not become a symbol; those who, under the guidance of the methods of their imperial masters, did not want any trace to remain, have discovered that although his tomb is unmarked, there are no remains, and there is no body, nevertheless a frightening opponent of imperialism, a symbol, a force, a presence that can never be destroyed, does exist.

When they hid Che's body they showed their weakness and their cowardice, because they also showed their fear of the example and the symbol. They did not want the exploited peasants, the workers, the students, the intellectuals, the democrats, the progressives, or the patriots of this hemisphere to have a place to go to pay tribute to Che. And in the world today, in which there is no specific place to go to pay tribute to Che's remains, tribute is paid to him everywhere. [*Applause*]

Today tribute is not paid to Che once a year, nor once every five, ten, fifteen, or twenty years; today homage is paid to Che every year, every month, every day, everywhere, in a factory, in a school, in a military barracks, in a home, among children, among Pioneers. Who can count how many millions of times in these twenty years the Pioneers have said: "Pioneers for communism, we will be like Che!" [*Applause*]

This one fact I've just mentioned, this one idea, this one custom in itself constitutes a great and permanent presence of Che. And I think that not only our Pioneers, not only our children, but children all over the hemisphere, all over the world could repeat this same slogan: "Pioneers for communism, we will be like Che!" [*Applause*]

Really, there can be no superior symbol, there can be no better image, there cannot be a more exact idea, when searching for the model revolutionary man, when searching for the model communist. I say this because I have the deepest conviction—I always have had and I still have today, just the same or more so than when I spoke that October 18 and I asked how we wanted our fighters, our revolutionaries, our party members, our children to be, and I said that we wanted them to be like Che. Because Che is the personification, Che is the image of that new man, the image of that human being if we want to talk about a communist society; [*Applause*] if our real objective is to build, not just socialism but the higher stages of socialism, if humanity is not going to renounce the lofty and extraordinary idea of living in a communist society one day.

If we need a paradigm, a model, an example to follow to attain these elevated ideas, then men like Che are essential, as are men and women who imitate him, who are like him, who think like him, who act like him; men and women whose conduct resembles his when it comes to doing their duty, in every little thing, every detail, every activity; in his attitude toward work, his habit of teaching and educating by setting an example;

his attitude of wanting to be first at everything, the first to volunteer for the most difficult tasks, the hardest ones, the most self-sacrificing ones; the individual who gives his body and soul to a cause, the individual who gives his body and soul to others, the person who displays true solidarity, the individual who never lets down a compañero; the simple man; the man without a flaw, who doesn't live any contradiction between what he says and what he does, between what he practices and what he preaches; a man of thought and a man of action—all of which Che symbolizes. [*Applause*]

For our country it is a great honor and privilege to have had Che as a son of our people even though he wasn't born in this land. He was a son because he earned the right to consider himself and to be considered a son of our country, and it is an honor and a privilege for our people, for our country, for our country's history, for our revolution to have had among its ranks a truly exceptional man such as Che.

That's not to say that I think exceptional people are rare; that's not to say that amid the masses there are not hundreds, thousands, even millions of exceptional men and women. I said it once during the bitter days after Camilo disappeared. When I recounted the history of how Camilo became the man he was, I said: "Among our people there are many Camilos." I could also say: "Among our peoples, among the peoples of Latin America and the peoples of the world there are many Ches."

But, why do we call them exceptional? Because, in actual fact, in the world in which they lived, in the circumstances in which they lived, they had the chance and the opportunity to demonstrate all that man, with his generosity and solidarity, is capable of being. And, indeed, seldom do ideal circumstances exist in which man has the opportunity to express himself and to show everything he has inside as was the case with Che.

Of course, it's clear that there are countless men and women among the masses who, partly as a result of other people's examples and certain new values, are capable of heroism, includ-

"Voluntary work was the brainchild of Che and one of the best things he left us during his stay in our country." *Fidel Castro, October 8, 1987.* Top, Guevara doing voluntary work; bottom, minibrigade members in Havana, 1988.

ing a kind of heroism I greatly admire: silent heroism, anonymous heroism, silent virtue, anonymous virtue. But given that it's so unusual, so rare for all the necessary circumstances to exist to produce a figure like Che—who today has become a symbol for the world, a symbol that will grow—it is a great honor and privilege that this figure was born during our revolution.

And as proof of what I said earlier about Che's presence and force today, I could ask: Is there a better date, a better anniversary than this one to remember Che with all our conviction and deep feelings of appreciation and gratitude? Is there a better moment than this particular anniversary, when we are in the middle of the rectification process?

What are we rectifying? We're rectifying all those things—and there are many—that strayed from the revolutionary spirit, from revolutionary work, revolutionary virtue, revolutionary effort, revolutionary responsibility; all those things that strayed from the spirit of solidarity among people. We're rectifying all the shoddiness and mediocrity that is precisely the negation of Che's ideas, his revolutionary thought, his style, his spirit, and his example.

I really believe, and I say it with great satisfaction, that if Che were sitting in this chair, he would feel jubilant. He would be happy about what we are doing these days, just like he would have felt very unhappy during that unstable period, that disgraceful period of building socialism in which there began to prevail a series of ideas, of mechanisms, of bad habits, which would have caused Che to feel profound and terrible bitterness. [*Applause*]

For example, voluntary work, the brainchild of Che and one of the best things he left us during his stay in our country and his part in the revolution, was steadily on the decline. It became a formality almost. It would be done on the occasion of a special date, a Sunday. People would sometimes run around and do things in a disorganized way.

The bureaucrat's view, the technocrat's view that voluntary

work was neither basic nor essential gained more and more ground. The idea was that voluntary work was kind of silly, a waste of time, that problems had to be solved with overtime, with more and more overtime, and this while the regular workday was not even being used efficiently. We had fallen into the bog of bureaucracy, of overstaffing, of work norms that were out of date, the bog of deceit, of untruth. We'd fallen into a whole host of bad habits that Che would have been really appalled at.

If Che had ever been told that one day, under the Cuban revolution there would be enterprises prepared to steal to pretend they were profitable, Che would have been appalled. Or if he'd been told of enterprises that wanted to be profitable and give out prizes and I don't know what else, bonuses, and they'd sell the materials allotted to them to build and charge as though they had built whatever it was, Che would have been appalled.

And I'll tell you that this happened in the fifteen municipalities in the capital of the republic, in the fifteen enterprises responsible for house repairs; and that's only one example. They'd appear as though what they'd produced was worth 8,000 pesos a year, and when the chaos was done away with, it turned out they were producing 4,000 pesos worth or less. So they were not profitable. They were only profitable when they stole.

Che would have been appalled if he'd been told that enterprises existed that would cheat to fulfill and even surpass their production plan by pretending to have done January's work in December.

Che would have been appalled if he'd been told that there were enterprises that fulfilled their production plan and then distributed prizes for having fulfilled it in monetary value but not in goods produced, and that engaged in producing items that meant more monetary value and refrained from producing others that yielded less profit, despite the fact that one item without the other was not worth anything.

Che would have been appalled if he'd been told that production norms were so slack, so weak, so immoral that on certain occasions almost all the workers fulfilled them two or three times over.

Che would have been appalled if he'd been told that money was becoming man's concern, man's fundamental motivation. He who warned us so much against that would have been appalled. Work shifts were being shortened and millions of hours of overtime reported; the mentality of our workers was being corrupted and men were increasingly being motivated by the pesos on their minds.

Che would have been appalled for he knew that communism could never be attained by wandering down those beaten capitalist paths and that to follow along those paths would mean eventually to forget all ideas of solidarity and even internationalism. To follow those paths would imply never developing a new man and a new society.

Che would have been appalled if he'd been told that a day would come when bonuses and more bonuses of all kinds would be paid, without these having anything to do with production.

Were he to have seen a group of enterprises teeming with two-bit capitalists—as we call them—playing at capitalism, beginning to think and act like capitalists, forgetting about the country, the people, and high standards (because high standards just didn't matter; all they cared about was the money being earned thanks to the low norms), he would have been appalled.

And were he to have seen that one day they would not just make manual work subject to [quantitative] production norms—which has a certain logic to it, like cutting cane and doing many other manual and physical activities—but even intellectual work, even radio and television work, and that here even a surgeon's work was likely to be subject to norms—putting just anybody under the knife in order to double or triple his income—I can truthfully say that Che would have been appalled, because none of those paths will ever lead us to communism. On the contrary, those paths lead to all the bad habits and the alienation of capitalism.

Those paths I repeat—and Che knew it very well—would never lead us to building real socialism, as a first and transitional stage to communism.

But don't think that Che was naive, an idealist, or someone out of touch with reality. Che understood and took reality into consideration. But Che believed in man. And if we don't believe in man, if we think that man is an incorrigible little animal, capable of advancing only if you feed him grass or tempt him with a carrot or whip him with a stick—anybody who believes this, anybody convinced of this will never be a revolutionary; anybody who believes this, anybody convinced of this will never be a socialist, anybody who believes this, anybody convinced of this will never be a communist. [*Applause*]

Our revolution is an example of what faith in man means because our revolution started from scratch, from nothing. We did not have a single weapon, we did not have a penny, even the men who started the struggle were unknown, and yet we confronted all that might, we confronted their hundreds of millions of pesos, we confronted the thousands of soldiers, and the revolution triumphed because we believed in man. Not only was victory made possible, but so was confronting the empire and getting this far, only a short way off from celebrating the twenty-ninth anniversary of the triumph of the revolution. How could we have done all this if we had not had faith in man?

Che had great faith in man. Che was a realist and did not reject material incentives. He deemed them necessary during the transitional stage, while building socialism. But Che attached more importance—more and more importance—to the conscious factor, to the moral factor.

At the same time, it would be a caricature to believe that Che was unrealistic and unfamiliar with the reality of a society and a people who had just emerged from capitalism.

But Che was mostly known as a man of action, a soldier, a leader, a military man, a guerrilla, an exemplary person who always was the first in everything; a man who never asked others

37

to do something that he himself would not do first; a model of a righteous, honest, pure, courageous man, full of human solidarity. These are the virtues he possessed and the ones we remember him by.

Che was a man of very profound thought, and he had the exceptional opportunity during the first years of the revolution to delve deeply into very important aspects of the building of socialism because, given his qualities, whenever a man was needed to do an important job, Che was always there. He really was a many-sided man and whatever his assignment, he fulfilled it in a completely serious and responsible manner.

He was in INRA [National Institute of Agrarian Reform] and managed a few industries under its jurisdiction at a time when the main industries had not yet been nationalized and only a few factories had been taken over. He headed the National Bank, another of the responsibilities entrusted to him, and he also headed the Ministry of Industry when this agency was set up. Nearly all the factories had been nationalized by then and everything had to be organized, production had to be maintained, and Che took on the job, as he had taken on many others. He did so with total devotion, working day and night, Saturdays and Sundays, at all hours, and he really set out to solve far-reaching problems. It was then that he tackled the task of applying Marxist-Leninist principles to the organization of production, the way he understood it, the way he saw it.

He spent years doing that; he spoke a lot, wrote a lot on all those subjects, and he really managed to develop a rather elaborate and very profound theory on the manner in which, in his opinion, socialism should be built leading to a communist society.

Recently, all these ideas were compiled, and an economist wrote a book that was awarded a Casa de las Américas prize. The author compiled, studied, and presented in a book the essence of Che's economic ideas, retrieved from many of his speeches and writings—articles and speeches dealing with a subject so decisive in the building of socialism. The name of the book is *The Economic Thought of Ernesto Che Guevara.** So much has been done to recall his other qualities that this aspect, I think, has been largely ignored in our country. Che held truly profound, courageous, bold ideas, which were different from many paths already taken.

In essence—in essence!—Che was radically opposed to using and developing capitalist economic laws and categories in building socialism. He advocated something that I have often insisted on: Building socialism and communism is not just a matter of producing and distributing wealth but is also a matter of education and consciousness. He was firmly opposed to using these categories, which have been transferred from capitalism to socialism, as instruments to build the new society.

At a given moment some of Che's ideas were incorrectly interpreted and, what's more, incorrectly applied. Certainly no serious attempt was ever made to put them into practice, and there came a time when ideas diametrically opposed to Che's economic thought began to take over.

This is not the occasion for going deeper into the subject. I'm essentially interested in expressing one idea: Today, on the twentieth anniversary of Che's death; today, in the midst of the profound rectification process we are all involved in, we fully understand that rectification does not mean extremism, that rectification cannot mean idealism, that rectification cannot imply for any reason whatsoever lack of realism, that rectification cannot even imply abrupt changes.

Starting out from the idea that rectification means, as I've said before, looking for new solutions to old problems, rectifying many negative tendencies that had been developing; that rectification implies making more accurate use of the system

* Published in English by Pathfinder under the title *Che Guevara: Economics and Politics in the Transition to Socialism* by Carlos Tablada.

and the mechanisms we have now, an Economic Management and Planning System which, as we said at the enterprises meeting, was a horse, a lame nag with many sores that we were treating with Mercurochrome and prescribing medicines for, putting splints on one leg, in short, fixing up the nag, the horse. I said that the thing to do now was to go on using that horse, knowing its bad habits, the perils of that horse, how it kicked and bucked, and try to lead it on our path and not go wherever it wishes to take us. I've said, let us take up the reins! [Applause]

These are very serious, very complicated matters and here we can't afford to take shots in the dark, and there's no place for adventures of any kind. The experience of so many years that quite a few of us have had the privilege of accumulating through a revolutionary process is worth something. And that's why we say now, we cannot continue fulfilling the plan simply in terms of monetary value; we must also fulfill it in terms of goods produced. We demand this categorically, and anyone who does otherwise must be quickly replaced, because there's no other choice! [Applause]

We maintain that all projects must be started and finished quickly so that there is never a repeat of what happened to us on account of the nag's bad habits: that business of doing the earthmoving and putting up a few foundations because that was worth a lot and then not finishing the building because that was worth little; that tendency to say, "I fulfilled my plan as to value but I didn't finish a single building," which made us waste hundreds of millions, billions, and we never finished anything.

It took fourteen years to build a hotel! Fourteen years wasting iron bars, sand, stone, cement, rubber, fuel, manpower before the country made a single penny from the hotel being used. Eleven years to finish our hospital here in Pinar del Río! It's true that in the end it was finished and it was finished well, but things of this sort should never happen again.

The minibrigades,* which were destroyed for the sake of such mechanisms, are now rising again from their ashes like a phoenix and demonstrating the significance of that mass movement, the significance of that revolutionary path of solving the problems that the theoreticians, technocrats, those who do not believe in man, and those who believe in two-bit capitalism had stopped and dismantled. This was how they were leading us into critical situations.

In the capital, where the minibrigades emerged, it pains us to think that over fifteen years ago we had found an excellent solution to such a vital problem, and yet they were destroyed in their peak moment. And so we didn't even have the manpower to build housing in the capital; and the problems kept piling up, tens of thousands of homes were propped up and were in danger of collapsing and killing people.

Now the minibrigades have been reborn and there are more than 20,000 minibrigade members in the capital. They're not in contradiction with the nag, with the Economic Management and Planning System, simply because the factory or workplace that sends them to the construction site pays them, but the state reimburses the factory or workplace for the salary of the minibrigade member. The difference is that whereas the worker would normally work five or six hours, on the minibrigade he works ten, eleven, or twelve hours doing the job of two or three men, and the enterprise saves money.

Our two-bit capitalist can't say his enterprise is being ruined. On the contrary, he can say, "They're helping the enterprise. I'm doing the job with thirty, forty, or fifty less men and spending less on wages." He can say, "I'm going to be profitable or at least lose less money; I'll distribute more prizes and bonuses since wage expenditures will be cut down." He organizes production

* The minibrigades are composed of workers from a particular workplace who volunteer to be relieved of their normal responsibilities for a period of time in order to build housing, schools, and day-care centers. They were discontinued in the mid-1970s and launched again in 1986.

better, he gets housing for his workers, who in turn are happier because they have new housing. He builds community projects such as special schools, polyclinics, day-care centers for the children of working women, for the family; in short, so many extremely useful things we are doing now and the state is building them without spending an additional cent in wages. That really is miraculous!

We could ask the two-bit capitalists and profiteers who have blind faith in the mechanisms and categories of capitalism: Could you achieve such a miracle? Could you manage to build 20,000 housing units in the capital without spending a cent more on wages? Could you build fifty day-care centers in a year without spending a cent more on wages, when only five had been included in the five-year plan and they weren't even built, and 19,500 mothers were waiting to get their children a place, which never materialized.

At that rate it would take 100 years! By then they would be dead, and fortunately so would all the technocrats, two-bit capitalists, and bureaucrats who obstruct the building of socialism. [*Applause*] They would have died without ever seeing day-care center number 100. Workers in the capital will have their 100 day-care centers in two years, and workers all over the country will have the 300 or so they need in three years. That will bring enrollment to 70,000 or 80,000 easily, without paying out an additional cent in wages or adding workers, because at that rate, with overstaffing everywhere, we would have ended up bringing workers in from Jamaica, Haiti, some Caribbean island, or some other place in the world. That was where we were heading.

It can be seen in the capital today that one in eight workers can be mobilized, I'm sure. This is not necessary because there would not be enough materials to give tasks to 100,000 people working in Havana, each one doing the work of three. We're seeing impressive examples of feats of work, and this is achieved by mass methods, by revolutionary methods, by communist methods, combining the interests of people in need with the interests of factories and those of society as a whole.

I don't want to become the judge of different theories, although I have my own theories and know what things I believe in and what things I don't and can't believe in. These questions are discussed frequently in the world today. And I only ask modestly, during this process of rectification, during this process and this struggle—in which we're going to continue as we already explained: with the old nag, while it can still walk, if it walks, and until we can cast it aside and replace it with a better horse, as I think that nothing is good if it's done in a hurry, without analysis and deep thought—What I ask for modestly at this twentieth anniversary is that Che's economic thought be made known; [*Applause*] that it be known here, in Latin America, in the world: in the developed capitalist world, in the Third World, and in the socialist world. Let it be known there too!

In the same way that we read many texts, of all varieties, and many manuals, Che's economic thought should be known in the socialist camp. Let it be known! [*Applause*] I don't say they have to adopt it, we don't have to get involved in that. Everyone must adopt the thought, the theory, the thesis they consider most appropriate, that which best suits them, as judged by each country. I absolutely respect the right of every country to apply the method or systems it considers appropriate; I respect it completely!

I simply ask that in a cultured country, in a cultured world, in a world where ideas are discussed, Che's economic theories should be made known. [*Applause*] I especially ask that our students of economics, of whom we have many and who read all kinds of pamphlets, manuals, theories about capitalist categories and capitalist laws, also begin to study Che's economic thought, so as to enrich their knowledge.

It would be a sign of ignorance to believe there is only one way of doing things, arising from the concrete experience of a specific time and specific historical circumstances. What I ask for, what I limit myself to asking for, is a little more knowledge, consisting of knowing about other points of view, points of view as respected, as deserving, and as coherent as Che's points of view. [*Applause*]

I can't conceive that our future economists, that our future generations will act, live, and develop like another species of little animal, in this case like the mule, who has those blinders only so that he can't see to either side; mules, furthermore, with grass and the carrot dangling in front as their only motivation. No, I would like them to read, not only to intoxicate themselves with certain ideas, but also to look at other ones, analyze them, and think about them.

Because if we were talking with Che and we said to him, "Look, all this has happened to us," all those things I was talking about before, what happened to us in construction, in agriculture, in industry, what happened in terms of the goods actually produced, work quality, and all that, Che would have said, "It's as I said, it's as I said." He'd have said, "It's as I warned, what's happening is exactly what I thought would happen," because that's simply the way it is. [*Applause*]

I want our people to be a people of ideas, of concepts. I want them to analyze those ideas, think about them, and, if they want, discuss them. I consider these things to be essential.

It might be that some of Che's ideas are closely linked to the initial stages of the revolution, for example his belief that when a quota was surpassed, the wages received should not go above that received by those on the scale immediately above. What Che wanted was for the worker to study, and he associated his concept with the idea that our people, who in those days had a very poor education and little technical expertise, should study. Today our people are much better educated, more cultured. We could discuss whether now they should earn as much as the next level or more. We could discuss questions associated with our reality of a far more educated people, a people far better prepared technically, although we must never give up the idea of constantly improving ourselves technically and educationally.

But many of Che's ideas are absolutely relevant today, ideas without which I am convinced communism cannot be built, like the idea that man should not be corrupted; that man should never be alienated; the idea that without consciousness, simply producing wealth, socialism as a superior society could not be built, and communism could never be built. [*Applause*]

I think that many of Che's ideas—many of his ideas!—have great relevance today. Had we known, had we learned about Che's economic thought we'd be a hundred times more alert, including in riding the horse, and whenever the horse wanted to turn right or left, wherever it wanted to turn—although, mind you, here this was without a doubt a right-wing horse—we should have pulled it up hard and got it back on the track, and whenever it refused to move, used the spurs hard. [*Applause*]

I think a rider, that is to say, an economist, that is to say, a party cadre, an administrative cadre, armed with Che's ideas would be better equipped to lead the horse along the right track.

Just being familiar with Che's thought, just knowing his ideas would enable him to say, "I'm doing badly here, I'm doing badly there, that's a consequence of this, that, or the other," provided that the system and mechanisms for building socialism and communism are really being developed and improved on.

I say this because it is my deepest conviction that if his thought remains unknown it will be difficult to get very far, to achieve real socialism, really revolutionary socialism, socialism with socialists, socialism and communism with communists. I'm absolutely convinced that ignoring those ideas would be a crime. That's what I'm putting to you.

We have enough experience to know how to do things; and there are extremely valuable principles of immense worth in Che's ideas and thought that simply go beyond the image that many people have of Che as a brave, heroic, pure man, of Che as a saint because of his virtues, as a martyr because of his selflessness and heroism. Che was also a revolutionary, a thinker, a man of doctrine, a man of great ideas, who was capable with great consistency of working out instruments and principles that unquestionably are essential to the revolutionary path.

Capitalists are very happy when they hear people talk about rent, profit, interest, bonuses, superbonuses; when they hear about markets, supply and demand as elements that regulate production and promote quality, efficiency, and all those things. For they say, "That's my kind of talk, that's my philosophy, that's my doctrine," and the emphasis that socialism may place on them makes them happy, for they know these are essential aspects of capitalist theory, laws, and categories.

We ourselves are being criticized by quite a few capitalists; they try to make people think that the Cuban revolutionaries are unrealistic, that the thing to do is go for all the lures of capitalism; that's where they aim their fire. But we'll see how far we get, even riding on the old nag full of sores, but correctly led, for as long as we don't have anything better than the old nag. We'll see how far we get in the rectification process with the steps we're taking now.

That's why on this, the twentieth anniversary, I'm making an appeal for our party members, our youth, our students, our economists to study and familiarize themselves with Che's political and economic thought.

Che is a figure with enormous prestige. Che is a figure whose influence will grow. Needless to say, those who feel frustrated or who dare to fight Che's ideas or use certain terms to describe Che or depict him as a dreamer, as someone who is out of touch with reality, do not deserve any revolutionary's respect. That's why we want our youth to have that instrument, to wield that weapon, even if for the time being it only serves to say, don't follow that mistaken path foreseen by Che; even if it only serves to increase our knowledge; even if it only serves to force us to meditate or to delve deeper into our revolutionary thought.

I sincerely believe that more than this ceremony, more than formal activities, more than all the honors, what we accomplish in action is really the best homage we can pay Che. The work spirit that is starting to appear in so many places and that is evident in so many examples in this province: those workers in Viñales who are working twelve and fourteen hours building minidams, starting them and finishing them one right after the other, and building them at half what they otherwise would have cost, with the result that in comparison with other projects—were we to use a capitalist term, although Che was opposed even to using capitalist terms when analyzing questions of socialism—were we to use the term profitability, we could say that those men on the minidam construction brigade working in Viñales are more than 100 percent profitable—more than 100 percent profitable! [*Applause*]

Che devoted absolute, total, priority attention to accounting, to analyzing expenditures and costs, cent by cent. Che could not conceive of building socialism and running the economy without proper organization, without efficient controls and strict accounting of every cent. Che could not conceive of development without an increase in labor productivity. He even studied mathematics to use mathematical formulas to implement controls and measure the efficiency of the economy. What's more, Che even dreamed of computers being used in running the economy as an essential, fundamental, and decisive way of measuring efficiency under socialism.

And those men I mentioned have made a contribution: for every peso spent they produce two; for every million pesos spent they produce two million. They and those working on the Guamá Dam, those working on the canal, those working on the thruway to Pinar del Río, those who are going to work on the Patate Dam, those who have started to work on roads and the waterworks in the city—there are a number of groups of workers who are carrying out real feats with pride, honor, discipline, loyalty to work. They are working with great productivity.

A few days ago we met with a group of construction workers building an avenue in the capital. They're all members of the party or the Union of Young Communists, or they're outstanding workers, about 200 men in all. Rather than linking their wages to production norms—I don't mean to say that this is negative, there are a number of fields where it is perfectly correct—since they move about in powerful trucks and machines, we don't have to tell them to work more but rather to work less. People like that are doing a lot, sometimes too much with too much effort. At times we'd have to tell them to take less trips because at the proper speed they can't make twenty-five trips with materials in a truck but twenty, because we don't want them to get killed. What we're interested in is not only what they do but the quality with which it is done. We told them we were much more interested in the quality than the quantity. [*Applause*] Quantity without quality is a waste of resources; it's throwing away work and materials.

Awareness of the need for water conservation, which had virtually died out in the shameful period when nothing was finished, is being regained, and the province of Pinar del Río is playing a leading role in this regard. [*Applause*]

The road brigades in the mountains of Pinar del Río are working with the same spirit, and the awareness of the need for water conservation is spreading all over the country along with the desire to build roads and highways and improve the efficiency of our economy, factories, agriculture, hospitals, and schools, to go full speed ahead with the economic and social development of the country.

Fortunately, during these years we have trained a large number of people with a high degree of technical knowledge and experience—university graduates and intermediate-level technicians. How does this compare to what we had in the early years of the revolution? When Che headed the Ministry of Industry, how many engineers did the country have, how many technicians, designers, researchers, scientists? Now we must have about twenty times the number we had then, perhaps more. If he had been able to draw on the collective experience of all the cadres that we have now, who knows what he could have accomplished.

Let's look at the medical sector alone. Back then we had 3,000 doctors and now we have 28,000. Each year our twenty-one medical schools graduate as many doctors as the total number in the country at that time. What a privilege! What a power! What force! As of next year we'll be graduating more doctors than those who stayed in the country in the early years. Can we or can we not do what we set our minds to in the field of public health? And what doctors they are! They work in the country-side, in the mountains, or in Nicaragua, Angola, Mozambique, Ethiopia, Vietnam, Kampuchea, or at the end of the world! Those are the doctors trained by the revolution! [*Applause*]

I'm sure Che would be proud, not of the shoddy things that have been done with such a two-bit profiteering mentality; he'd be proud of the knowledge and technology our people have, of our teachers who went to Nicaragua and the 100,000 who of-fered to go. He'd be proud of our doctors willing to go anywhere in the world, of our technicians, of our hundreds of thousands of compatriots who have been on internationalist missions! [*Ap-plause*]

I'm sure Che would be proud of that spirit just like we all are, but we cannot permit what we have built with our heads and hearts to be trampled on with our feet. [*Applause*] That's the point, that and the fact that with all the resources that we have built up, with all that force, we should be able to advance and take advantage of all the potential opened up by socialism and the revolution to get people to move ahead. I would like to know if the capitalists have people like those I mentioned.

They are extraordinary internationalists and workers; you have to talk to them to see how they think and feel, to see how deeply they love their work, and this is not because they're workaholics but because they feel the need to make up for lost time, time lost during the revolution, time lost during almost 60 years of neocolonial republic, time lost during centuries of colo-nialism.

We must regain this time! And hard work is the only way, not waiting 100 years to build 100 day-care centers in the capital when we can really do it in two; not waiting 100 years to build 350 all over the country when we can do it in three with our work; not waiting 100 years to solve the housing problem when we can do it in a few years with our work, our stones, our sand, our materials, our cement, even with our oil and steel produced by our workers.

As I said this afternoon at the hospital ceremony, the year 2000 is just around the corner. We must set ourselves ambitious goals for the year 2000, not for the year 3000 or 2100 or 2050, and if someone suggests that we should, we must reply: "That may suit you but not us! We have the historic mission of building a new country, a new society, the historic mission of making a revolution and developing a country; those of us who have had the honor and privilege of not just promoting development but a socialist development and working for a more humane and advanced society."

To those who encourage laziness and frivolity we will say, "We will live longer than you, not just better than you, or like we would live if everyone were like you. We will live longer than you and be healthier than you because with your laziness you will be sedentary and obese, you will have heart problems, circulatory ailments, and all sorts of other things, because work doesn't harm your health, work promotes health, work safeguards health, and work created man."

These men and women doing great things must become models. We could say that they're being true to the motto, "We will be like Che!" They are working like Che worked or as Che would have worked. [Applause]

When we were discussing where this ceremony should be held, there were many possible places. It could have been in the Plaza of the Revolution in the capital, it could have been in a province, it could have been in one of the many workplaces or factories that the workers wanted to name after Che.

We gave the matter some thought and recalled this new and important factory, the pride of Pinar del Río, the pride of the country and example of what can be done with progress, study, education in this province, which in the past was so neglected and backward and now has young workers capable of running such a complex and sophisticated factory. We need only say that the rooms where the circuits are printed must be ten times cleaner than an operating room to meet the required standard. It was necessary to do such complex work, with such quality and good equipment, and Pinar del Río residents are doing it marvelously. [*Applause*]

When we toured it we were deeply impressed and we talked with many compañeros, the members of the Central Committee, about what you were doing in the factory; in the machine industry, which is advancing at a rapid pace; what was being done in construction. We realized the great future of this factory as a manufacturer of components, of vanguard technology, which will have a major impact on development and productivity, on the automation of production processes.

When we toured your first-rate factory and saw the ideas you had which are being put into practice, we realized it will become a huge complex of many thousands of workers, the pride of the province and the pride of the country. In the next five years more than 100 million pesos will be invested in it to make it a real giant. When we learned that the workers wanted to name it after Che because he was so concerned with electronics, computers, and mathematics, the leadership of our party decided that this was where the ceremony marking the twentieth anniversary of Che's death should be held, [*Applause*] and that the factory should be given the glorious and beloved name of Ernesto Che Guevara. [*Applause*]

I know that its workers, its young workers, its dozens and dozens of engineers, its hundreds of technicians will do honor to that name and work as they should. This doesn't only mean being here fourteen, twelve, or ten hours, for often on certain jobs eight hours of work well done is a real feat. We've seen compañeros, especially many women workers doing microsoldering, which is really difficult work that requires rigor and tremendous concentration. We've seen them, and it's hard to imagine how these compañeras can spend eight hours doing that work and turn out up to 5,000 units daily.

Compañeros, don't think that we feel that the only way to solve problems is to work twelve or fourteen hours a day. There are jobs where you can't work twelve or fourteen hours. In some even eight hours can be a lot. One day we hope that not all workdays will be the same. We hope that in certain fields—if we have enough personnel, and we will if we employ them efficiently—we can have six-hour workdays.

What I mean to say is that being true to Che's example and name also means using the workday with the right pace, being concerned about high standards, having people do various tasks, avoiding overstaffing, working in an organized manner, and developing consciousness.

I'm sure that the workers of this factory will be worthy of Che's name, [*Applause*] just as I'm sure that this province was deserving of hosting the anniversary and will continue to be deserving.

If there is something left to say tonight it's that despite our problems; despite the fact that we have less hard currency than ever before, for reasons we have explained in the past; despite the drought; despite the intensification of the imperialist blockade—as I see our people respond, as I see more and more possibilities open up, I feel confident, I feel optimistic, and I am absolutely convinced that we will do everything we set our minds to! [*Applause*]

We'll do it with the people, with the masses; we'll do it with the principles, pride, and honor of each and every one of our party members, workers, youth, peasants, and intellectuals!

I can proudly say that we are giving Che well-deserved tribute and honor, and if he lives more than ever, so will the homeland! If he is an opponent of imperialism more powerful than ever, the homeland will also be more powerful than ever against imperialism and its rotten ideology! [*Applause*] And if one day we chose the path of revolution, of socialist revolution and of communism, the path of building communism, today we are prouder to have chosen that path because it is the only one that can give rise to men like Che and a people composed of millions of men and women capable of being like Che! [*Applause*]

As [José] Martí said, whereas there are men without dignity, there are also men who carry inside them the dignity of many men! We might add that there are men who carry inside them the dignity of the world, and one of those men is Che!

Patria o muerte! [Homeland or death]

Venceremos! [We will win] [*Ovation*]

Ernesto Che Guevara

Ernesto "Che" Guevara was born in Argentina in 1928. While living in Guatemala in 1954, he was an eyewitness to the CIA's successful overthrow of the elected government of Jacobo Arbenz. Later he went to Mexico, where he joined Fidel Castro and other Cuban revolutionaries seeking to overthrow dictator Fulgencio Batista.

In December 1956 Guevara was part of the expedition that landed in Cuba aboard the yacht *Granma* to begin the guerrilla struggle. Originally the troop doctor, Guevara eventually became a commander of the Rebel Army.

Following the rebels' victory on January 1, 1959, Guevara became a central leader of the new revolutionary government. He held a number of posts, including president of the National Bank and minister of industry, and was a leading Cuban representative at the United Nations and other world forums.

In 1965 Guevara left Cuba to participate directly in revolutionary struggles abroad. He initially went to the Congo and later to Bolivia, where he led a guerrilla movement against that country's military dictatorship. Wounded and captured by the Bolivian army in a CIA-organized operation on October 8, 1967, he was murdered the following day.

Fidel Castro

Born in eastern Cuba in 1926, Fidel Castro became active politically while attending the University of Havana in the mid-1940s.

After Fulgencio Batista's coup d'état of March 10, 1952, Castro organized a revolutionary movement to initiate armed struggle against the U.S. backed dictatorship. On July 26, 1953, he led an unsuccessful attack on the Moncada army garrison in Santiago de Cuba. Many participants were captured and murdered in cold blood; Castro and other survivors were imprisoned. Originally sentenced to fifteen years, he was released in 1955 together with his comrades as a result of an amnesty campaign. Following his release, he formed the July 26 Movement.

In July 1955 Castro left Cuba for Mexico, where he organized a guerrilla expedition to return to Cuba. On December 2, 1956, along with eighty-one other fighters, Castro landed in southeastern Cuba aboard the yacht *Granma*. For the next two years, he directed the operations of the Rebel Army from its base in the Sierra Maestra mountains. On January 1, 1959, Batista was forced to flee Cuba and shortly thereafter Rebel Army units entered Havana.

In February 1959 Castro became prime minister, a position he held until December 1976, when he became president of the Council of State and Council of Ministers. He has been commander in chief of Cuba's armed forces since 1959 and is first secretary of the Central Committee of the Communist Party of Cuba.

The Cuban Revolution

From the Escambray to the Congo
In the Whirlwind of the Cuban Revolution
Interview with Víctor Dreke

In this participant's account, Víctor Dreke describes how easy it became after the Cuban Revolution to "take down the rope" segregating blacks from whites at town dances, yet how enormous was the battle to transform social relations underlying all the "ropes" inherited from capitalism and Yankee domination. He recounts the determination, internationalism, and creative joy with which working people have defended their revolutionary course against U.S. imperialism—from Cuba's own Escambray mountains, to the Americas, Africa, and beyond. $17 Also in Spanish.

Dynamics of the Cuban Revolution
A Marxist Appreciation
Joseph Hansen
How did the Cuban Revolution come about? Why does it represent, as Hansen puts it, an "unbearable challenge" to U.S. imperialism? What political challenges has it confronted?
Written as the revolution advanced from its earliest days. $22.95

Making History
*Interviews with Four Generals of
Cuba's Revolutionary Armed Forces*
Through the stories of four Cuban generals—three of them leaders of the Cuban forces at Playa Girón that defeated the invaders in less than 72 hours—we can see the class dynamics that have shaped our entire epoch. We can understand how the people of Cuba, as they struggle to build a new society, have for more than forty years held Washington at bay. $15.95 Also in Spanish.

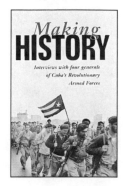

in today's world

To Speak the Truth
Why Washington's 'Cold War' against Cuba Doesn't End

Fidel Castro and Che Guevara

In historic speeches before the United Nations and UN bodies, Guevara and Castro address the workers of the world, explaining why the U.S. government so hates the example set by the socialist revolution in Cuba and why Washington's efforts to destroy it will fail. $17

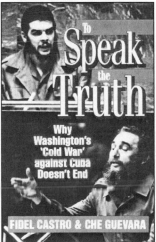

Che Guevara Talks to Young People

"If this revolution is Marxist, it is because it discovered by its own methods the road pointed out by Marx." Ernesto Che Guevara, 1960. Eight speeches from 1959 to 1964 by the legendary Argentine-born leader of the Cuban Revolution. Preface by Armando Hart, introduction by Mary-Alice Waters. $15 Also in Spanish.

Cuba and the Coming American Revolution

Jack Barnes

"There will be a victorious revolution in the United States before there will be a victorious counterrevolution in Cuba." That statement, made by Fidel Castro in 1961, remains as accurate today as when it was spoken. This is a book about the class struggle in the United States, where the revolutionary capacities of workers and farmers are today as utterly discounted by the ruling powers as were those of the Cuban toilers. And just as wrongly. It is about the example set by the people of Cuba that revolution is not only necessary—it can be made. $13

www.pathfinderpress.com

Also from Pathfinder

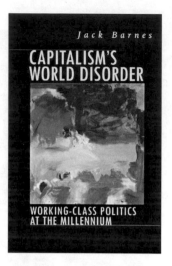

Capitalism's World Disorder
Working-Class Politics at the Millennium
JACK BARNES

The social devastation and financial panic, the coarsening of politics and politics of resentment, the cop brutality and acts of imperialist aggression accelerating around us—all are the product not of something gone wrong but of the lawful workings of capitalism. Yet the future can be changed by the united struggle and selfless action of workers and farmers conscious of their power to transform the world. $24 Also in Spanish and French.

Cosmetics, Fashions, and the Exploitation of Women
JOSEPH HANSEN, EVELYN REED, AND MARY-ALICE WATERS

How big business plays on women's second-class status and social insecurities to market cosmetics and rake in profits. The introduction by Waters explains how the entry of millions of women into the workforce during and after World War II irreversibly changed U.S. society and laid the basis for a renewed rise of struggles for women's emancipation. $15

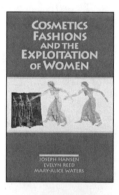

Malcolm X Talks to Young People
Four talks and an interview given to young people in Ghana, the United Kingdom, and the United States in the last months of Malcolm's life. This new edition contains the entire December 1964 presentation by Malcolm X at the Oxford Union in the United Kingdom, in print for the first time anywhere. The collection concludes with two memorial tributes by a young socialist leader to this great revolutionary. With a new preface and an expanded photo display of 17 pages. $15